SAIA

ONLY
45

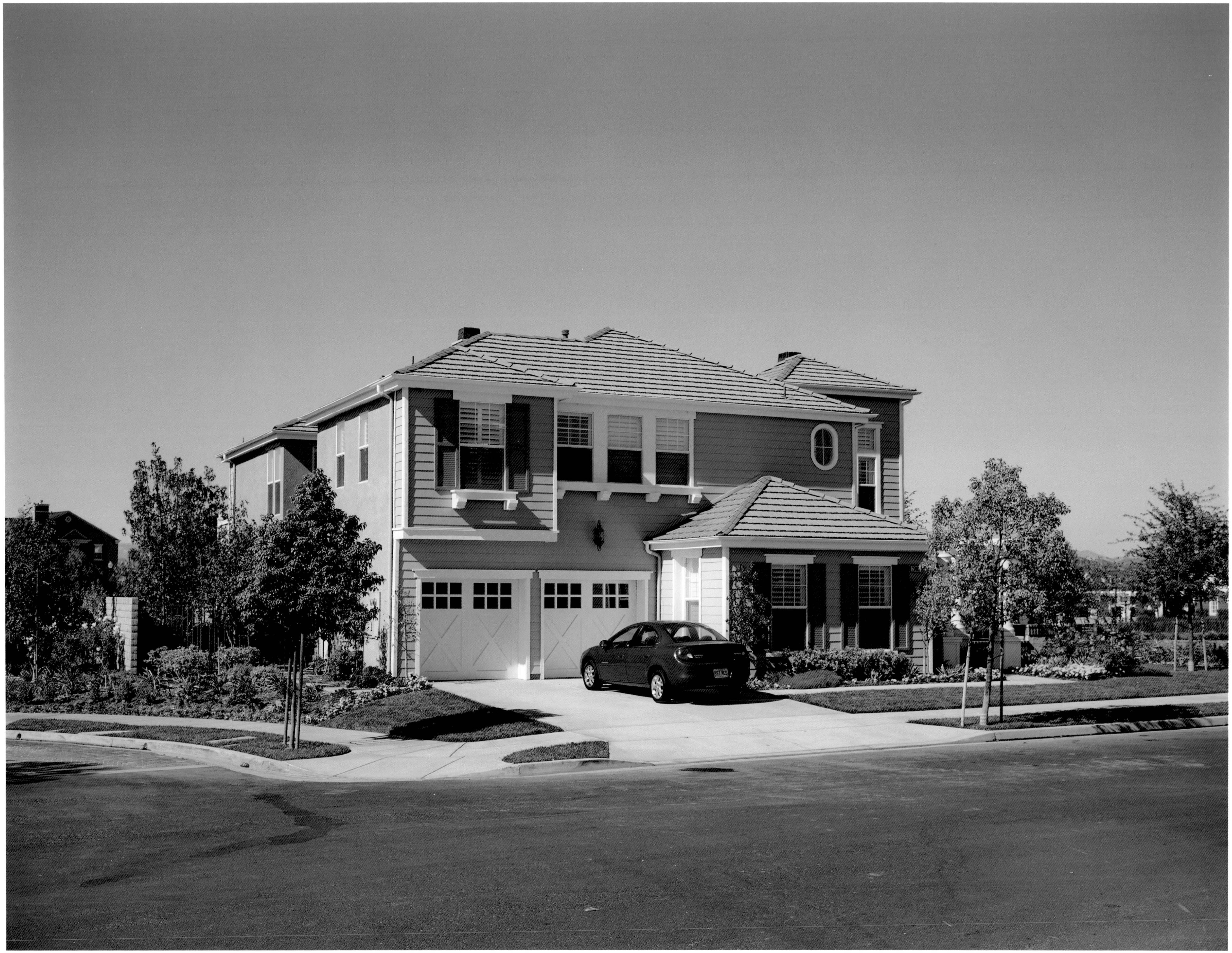

EAST

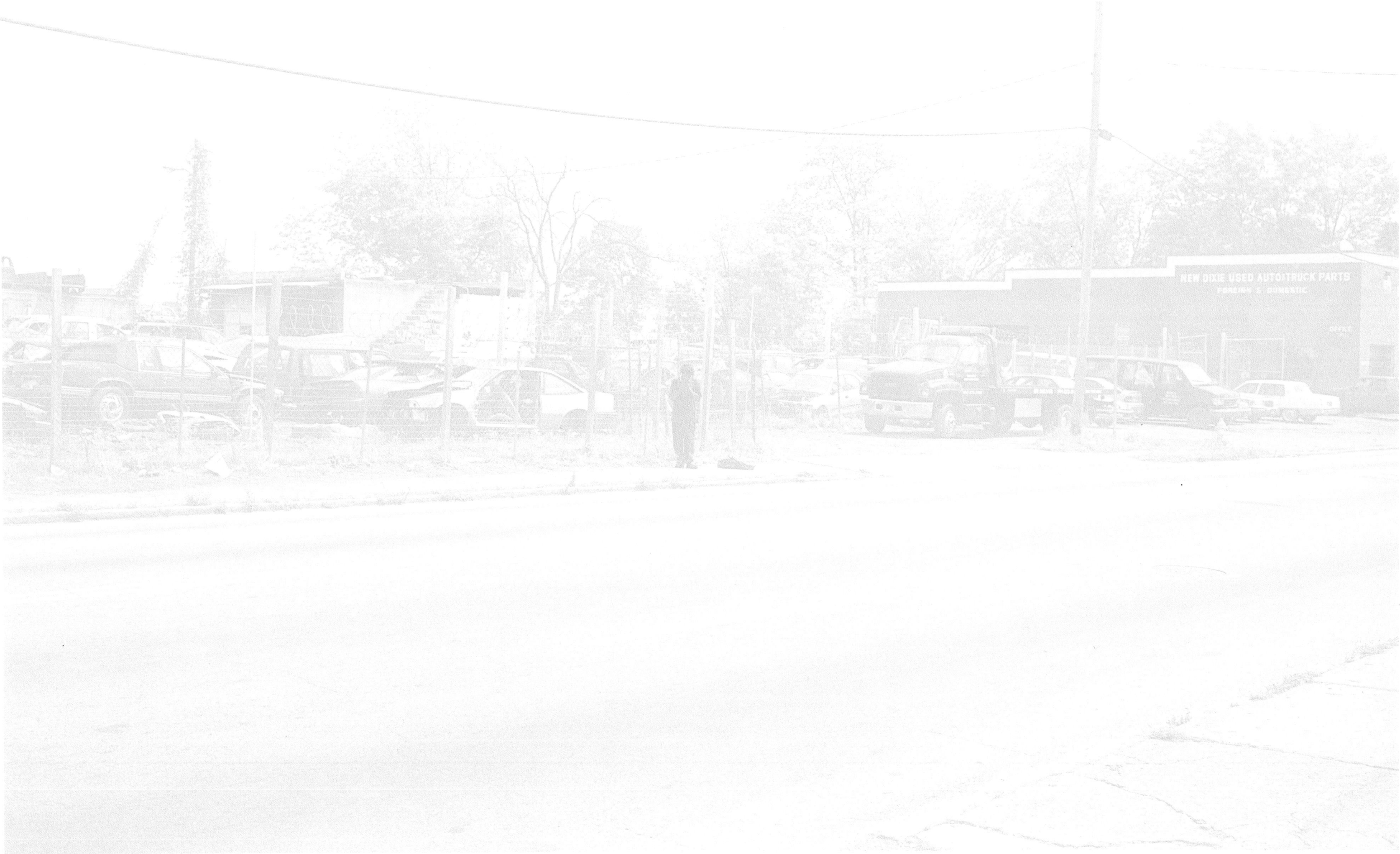
NEW DIXIE USED AUTO&TRUCK PARTS
FOREIGN & DOMESTIC
OFFICE

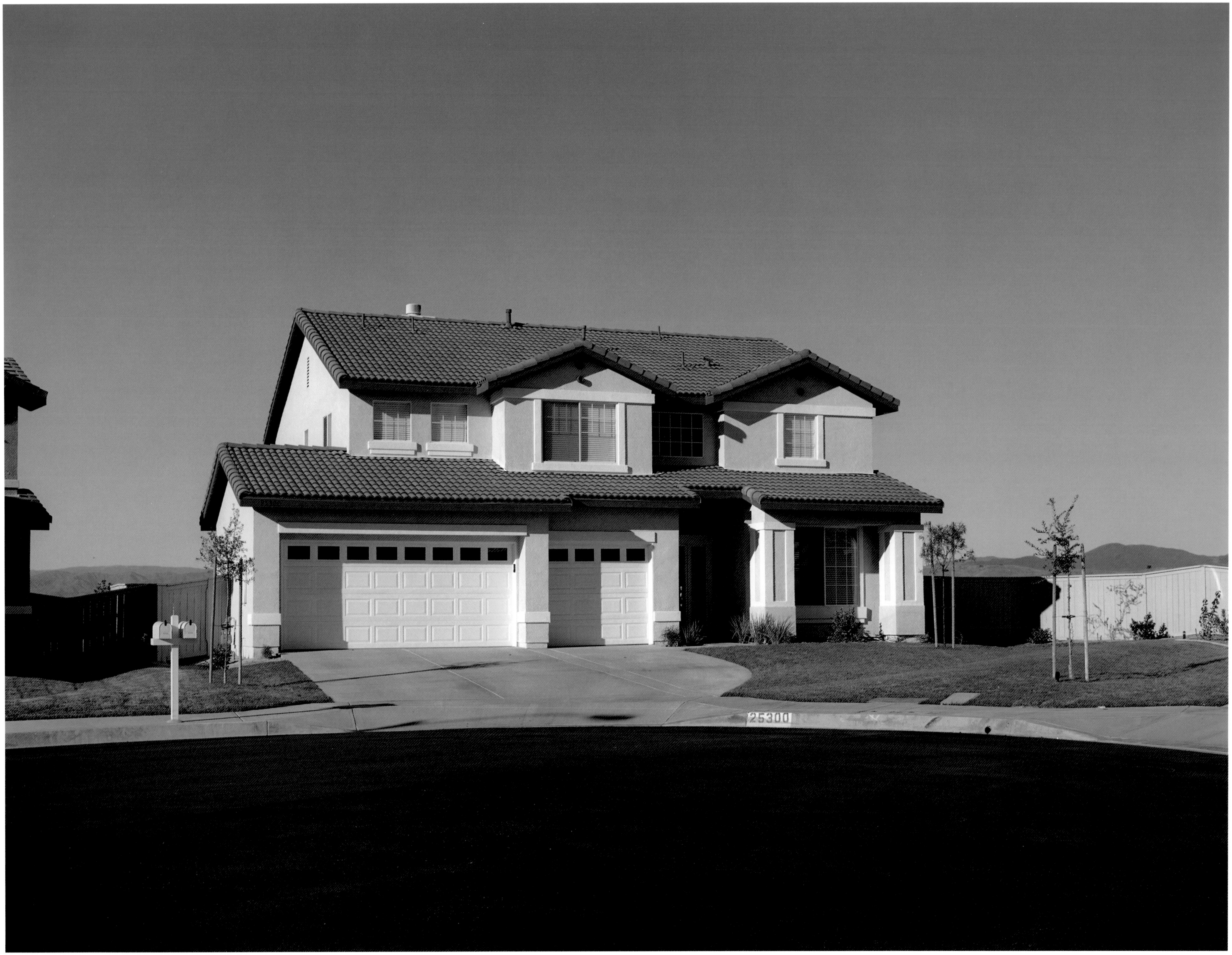
25300

FIFE
CLEANERS
BEAUTY SALON

YUM-YUM

WELCOME
OPEN for
BUSINESS

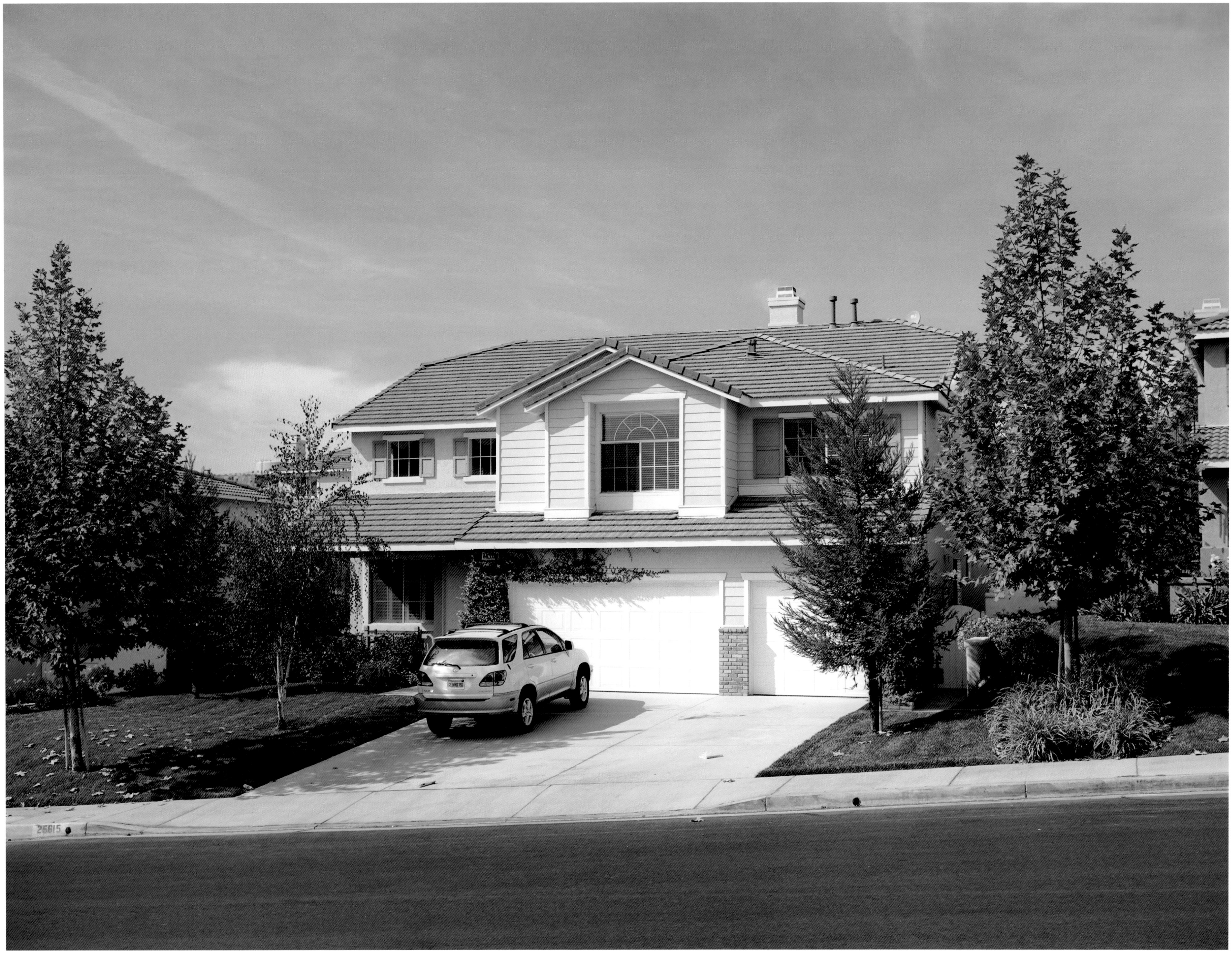
25615

MAYFIELD FOODS
CHECKS CASHED
FAMILY

1/2 THE PRICE
AOL!

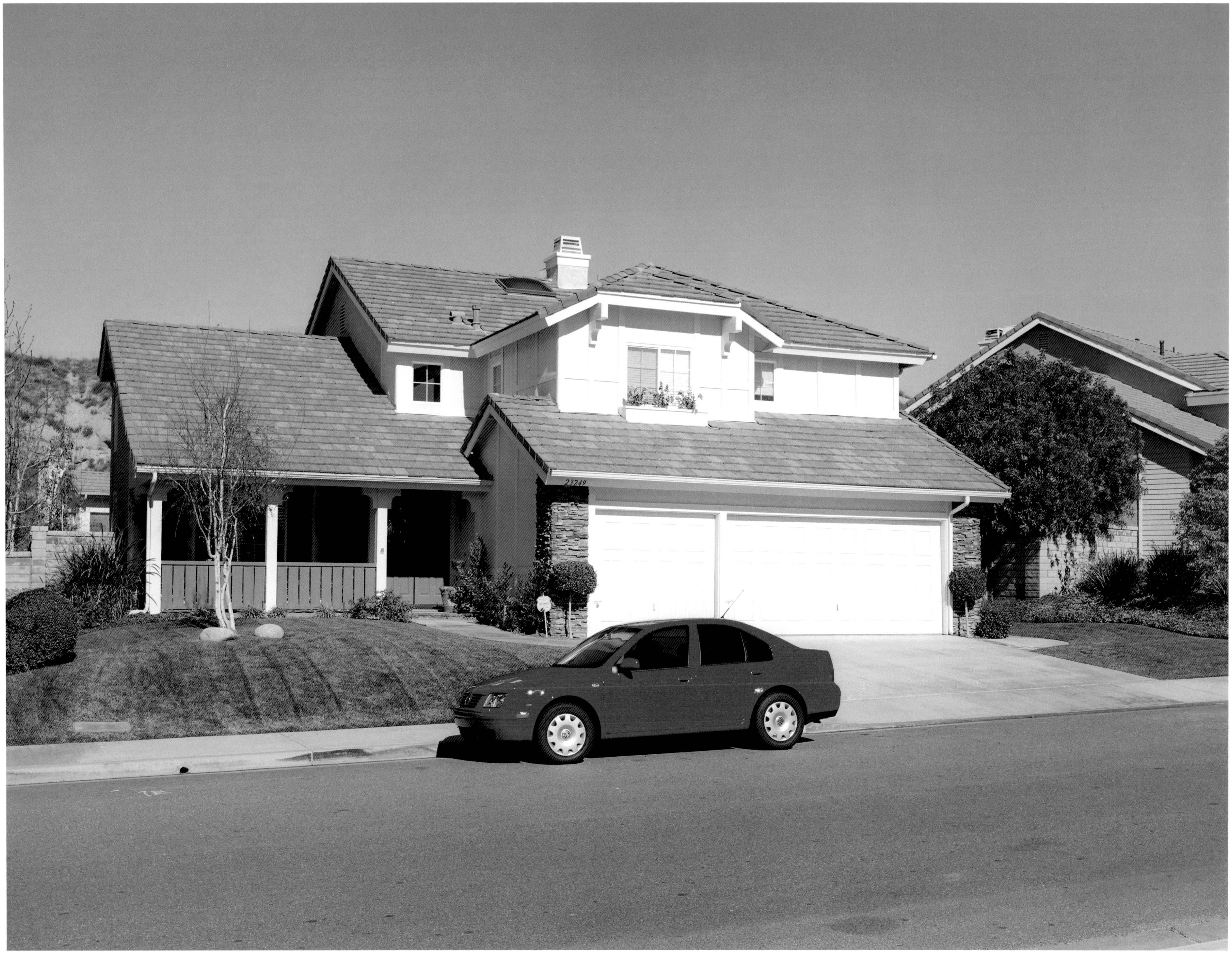
23249

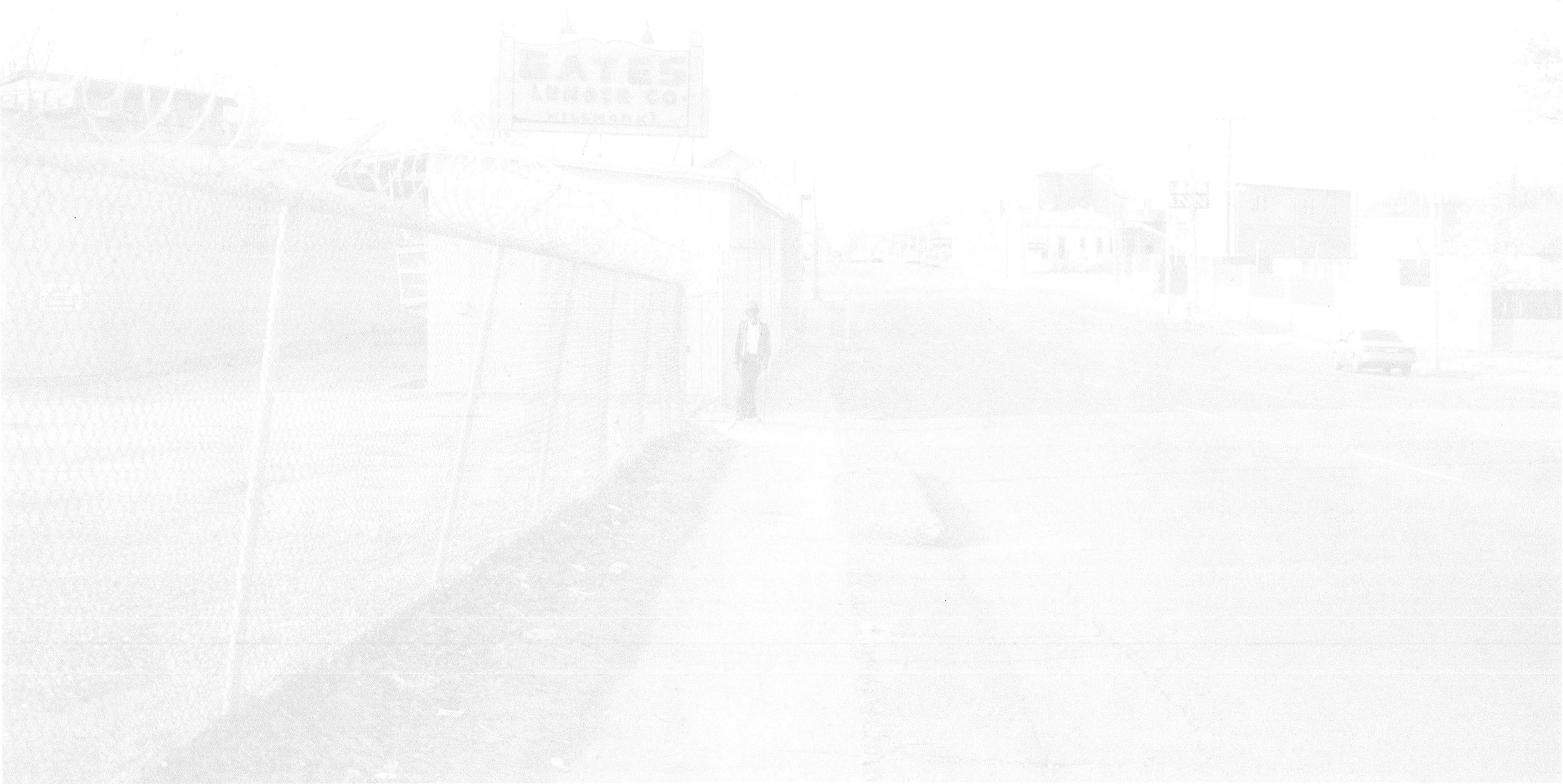
GATES
LUMBER CO
INN

S ACCEPTED
ONLY
BANK

DON'S & BEN'S
U.S
NAILS
TEL:354-0257
For Information
Wade
Interests
490-9000
LIQUOR

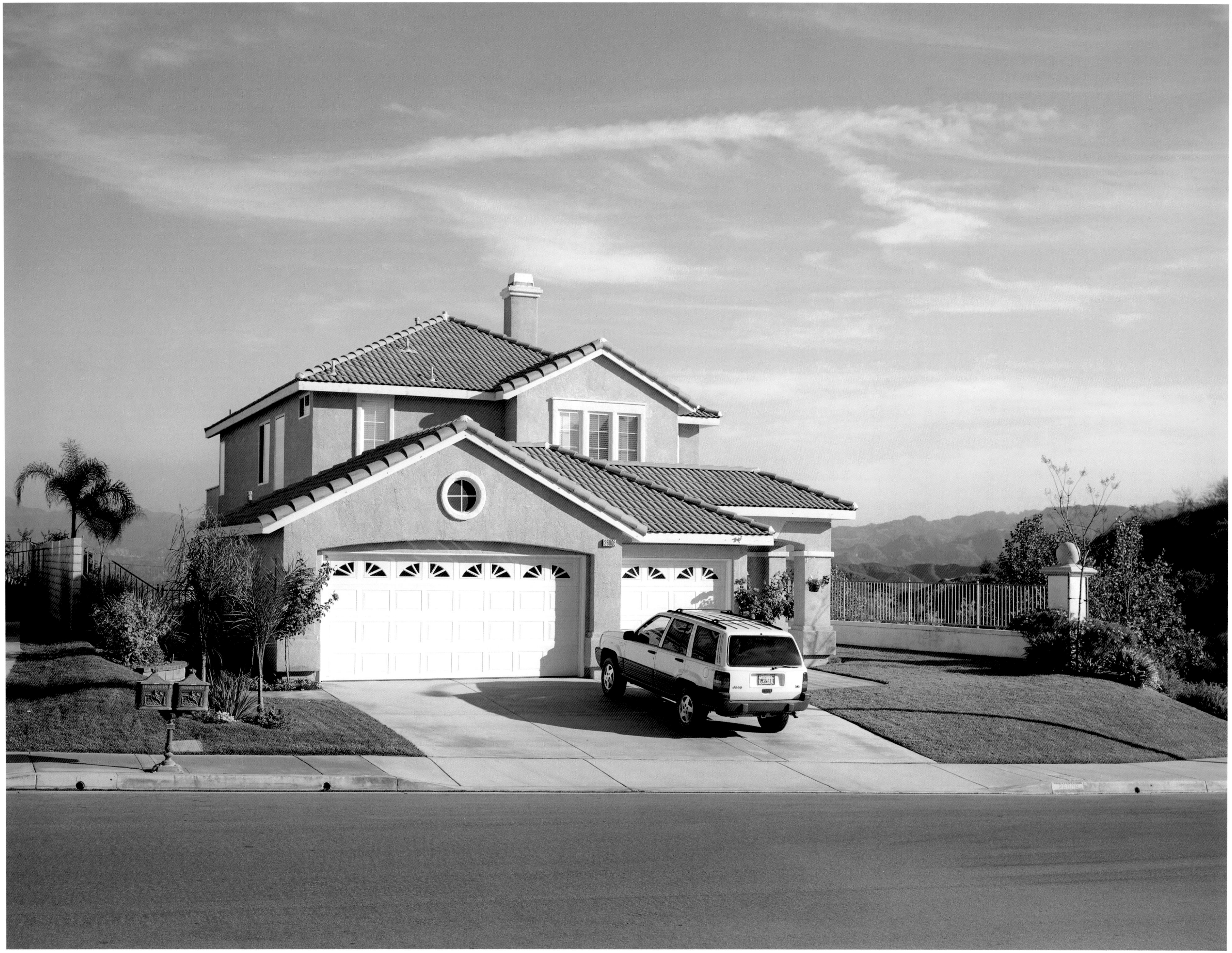

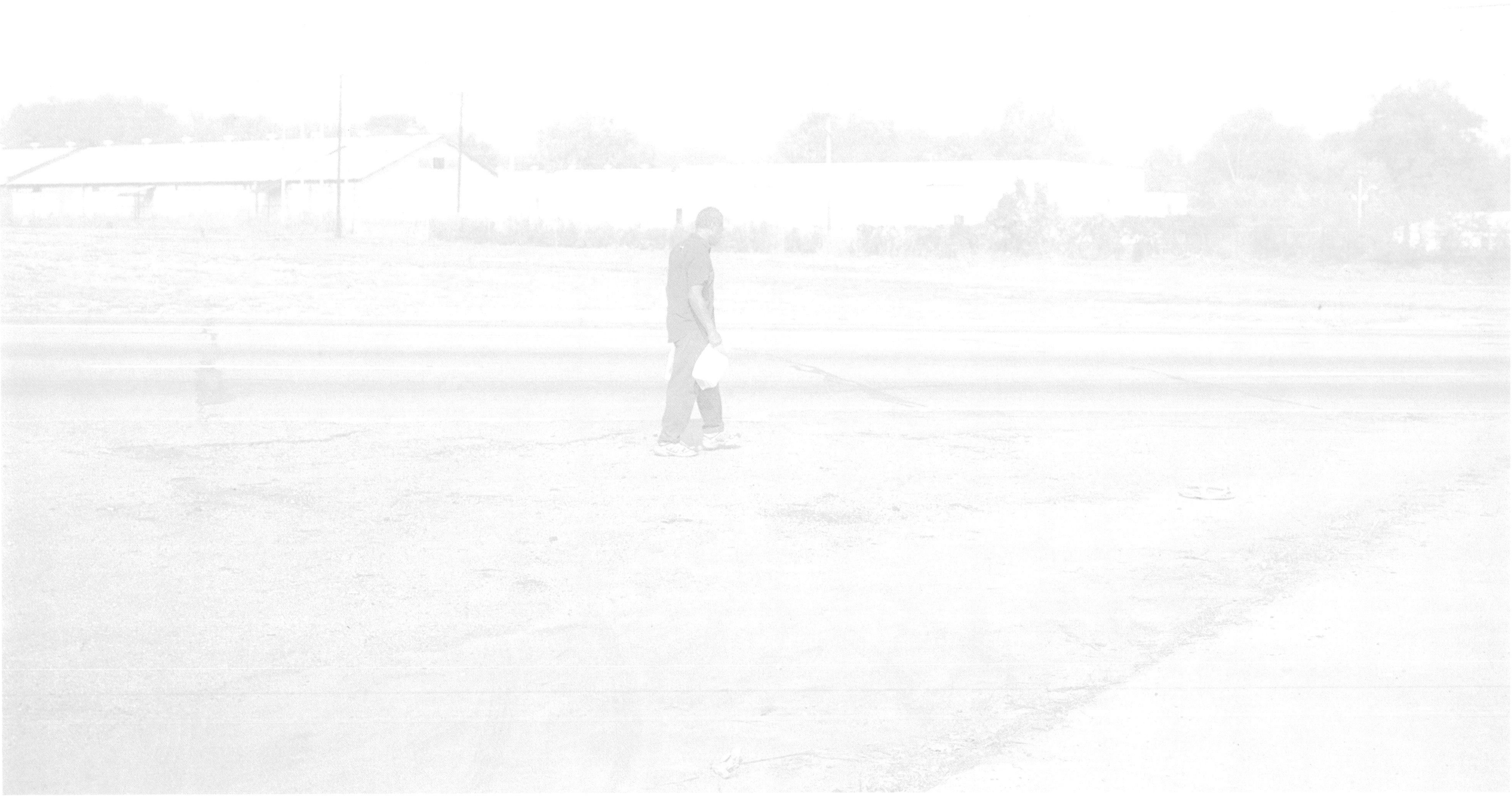

Guilford Technical
Community College
SPEED
LIMIT
35

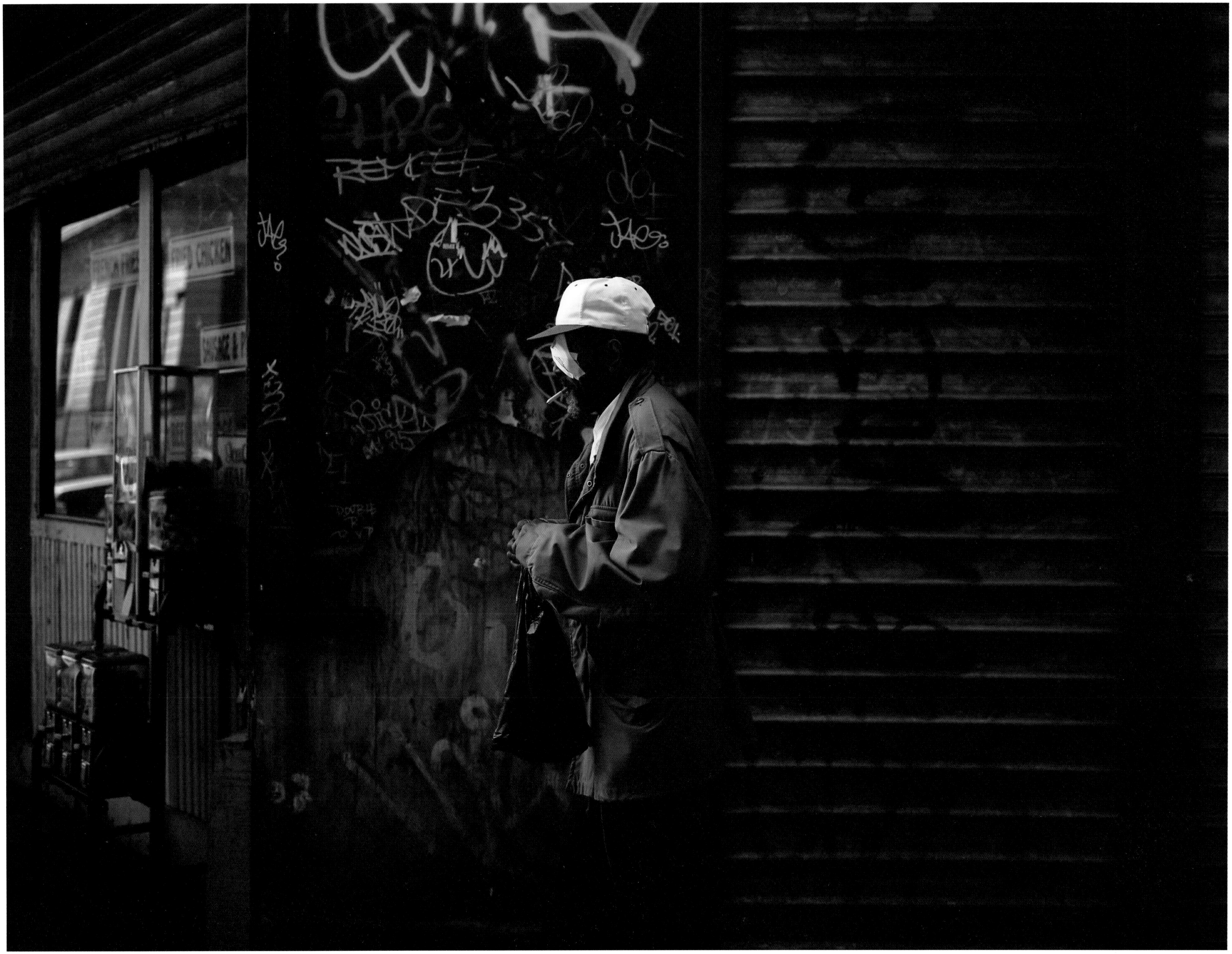
FRIED CHICKEN

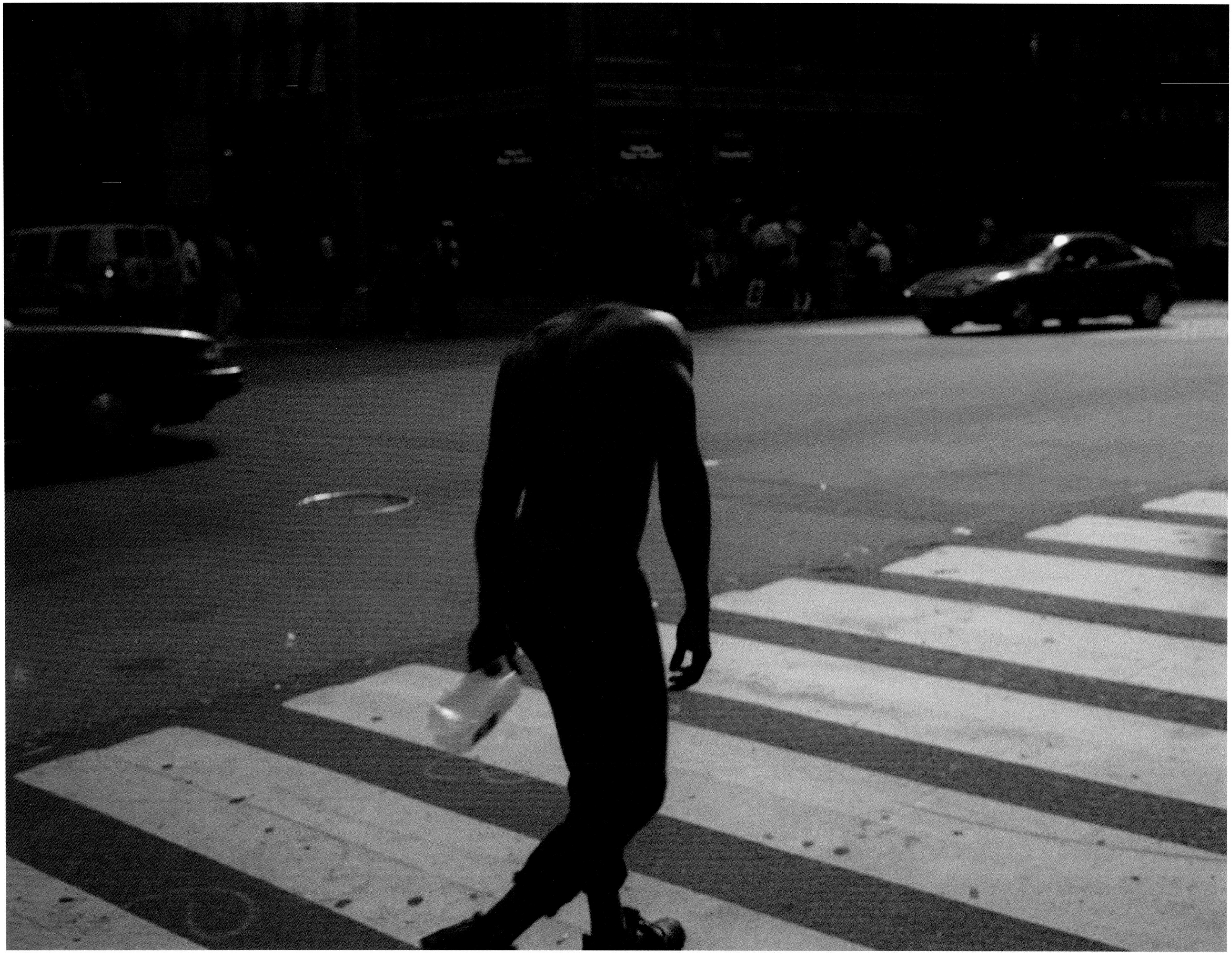

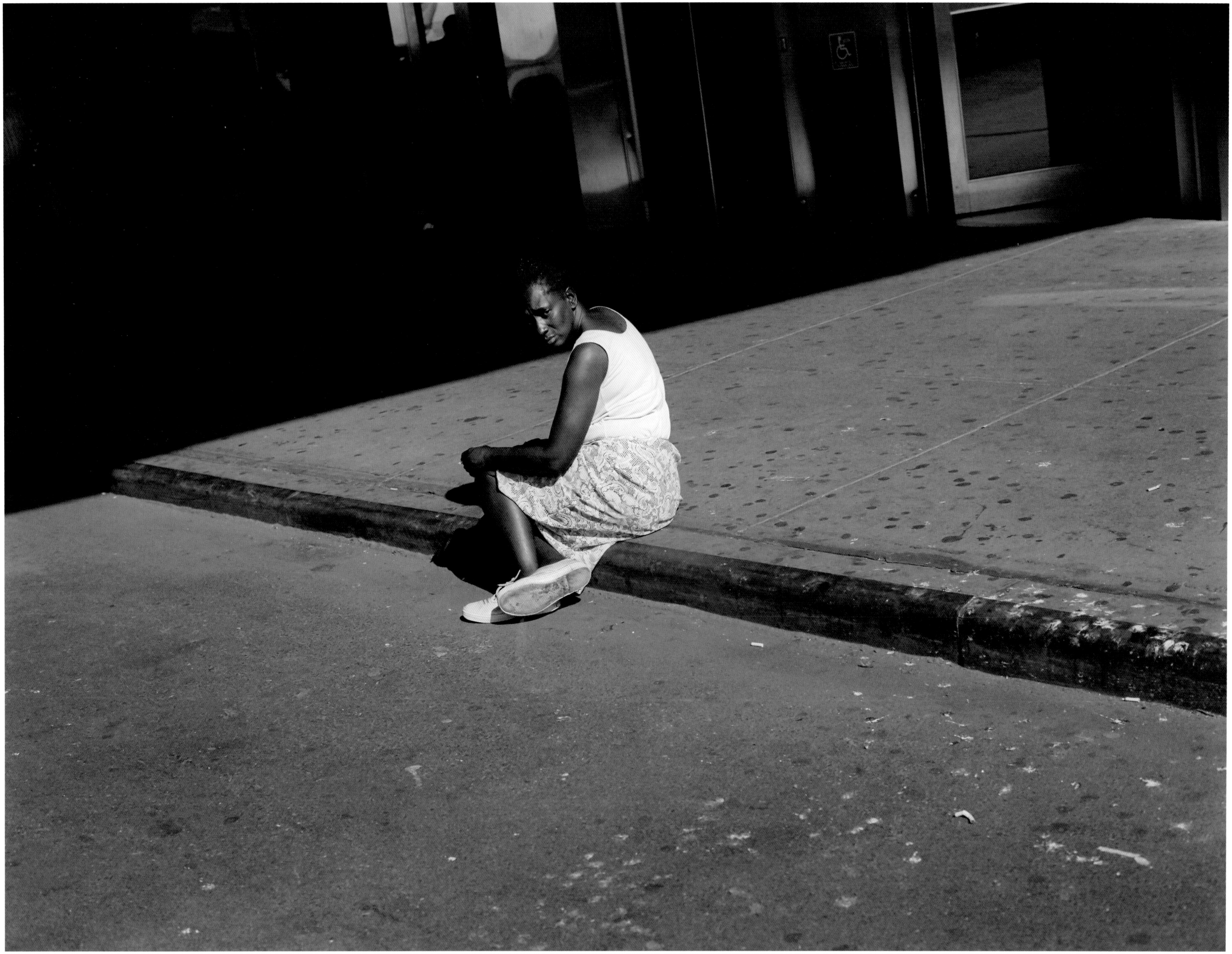

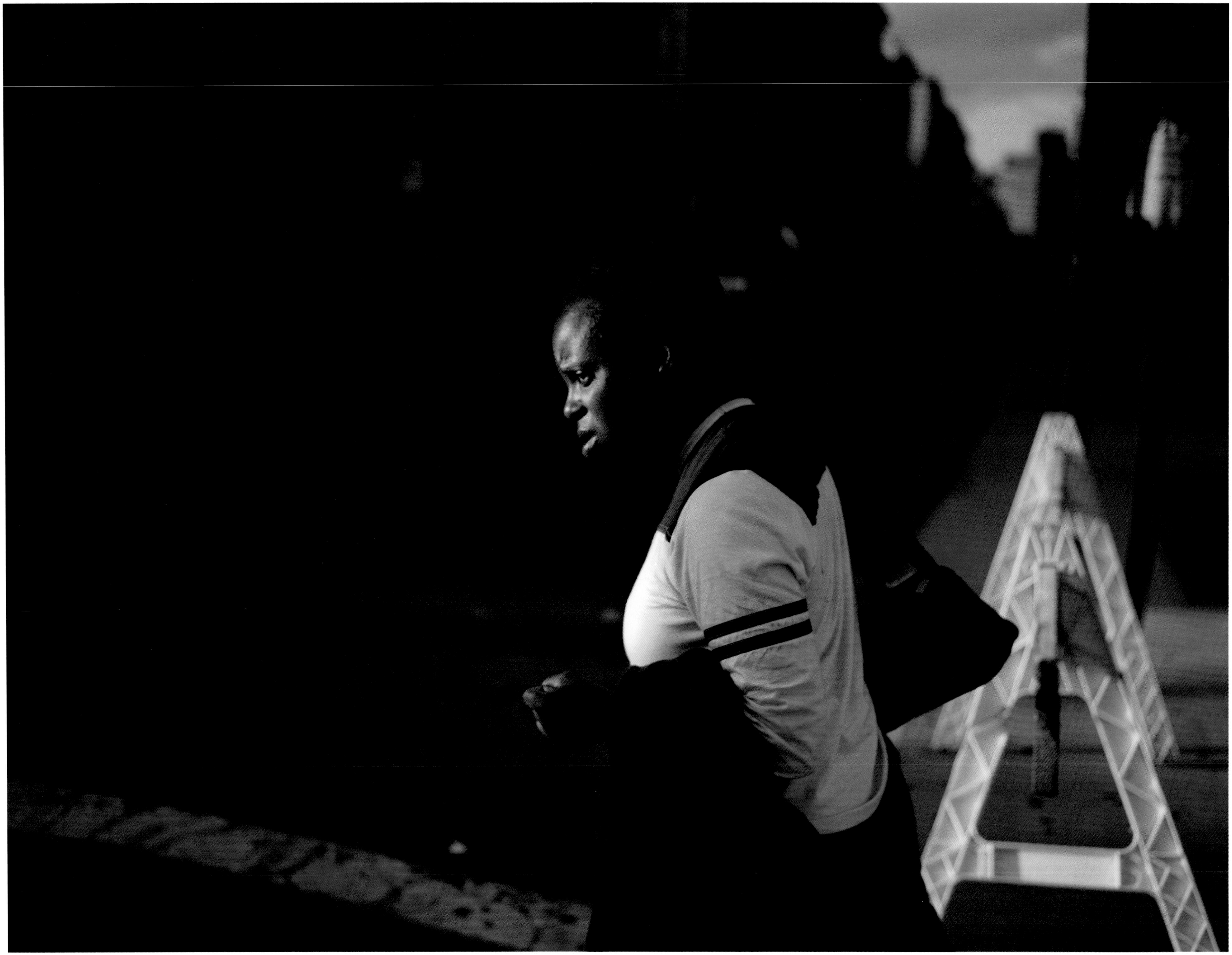

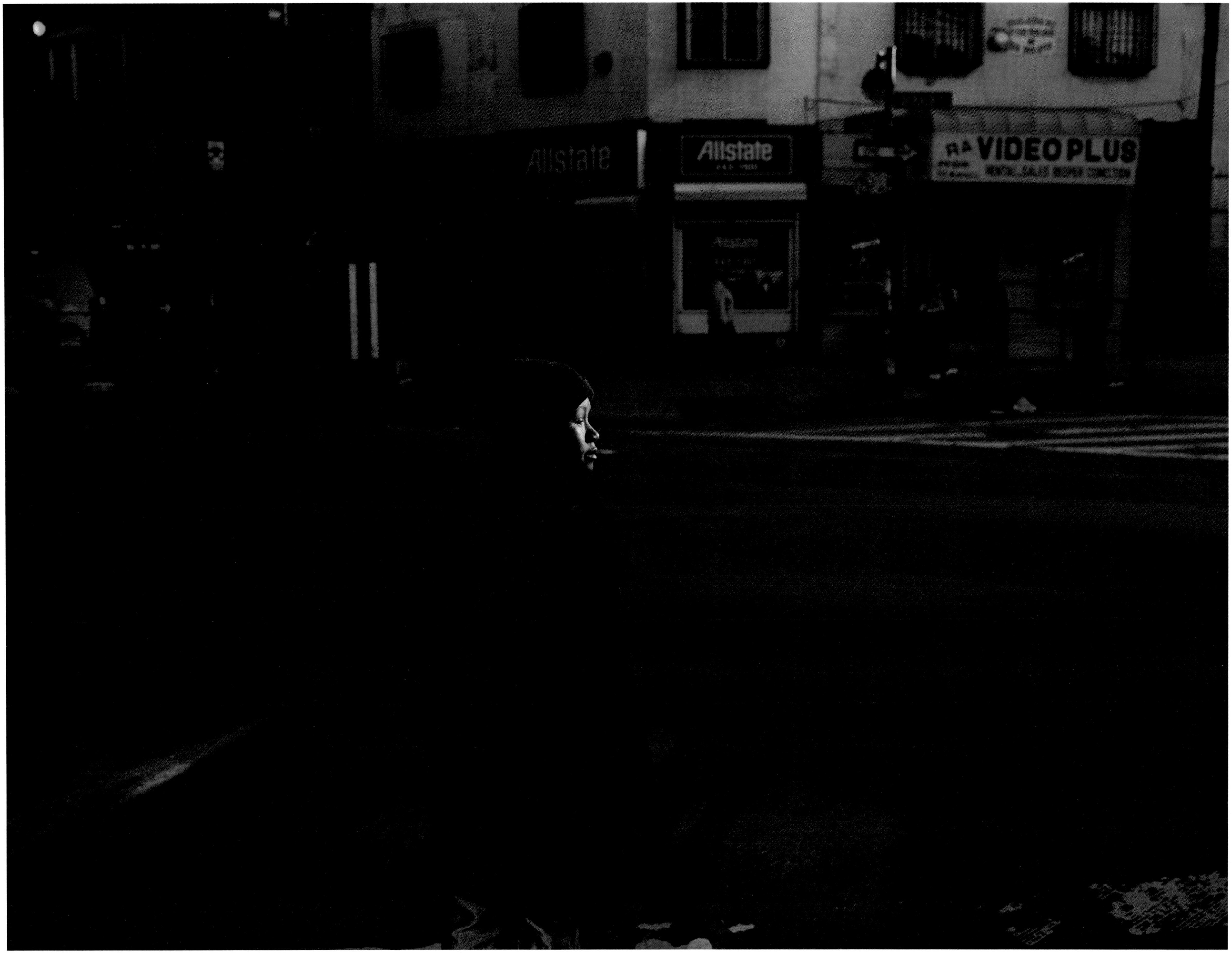
Allstate
Allstate
RA VIDEOPLUS

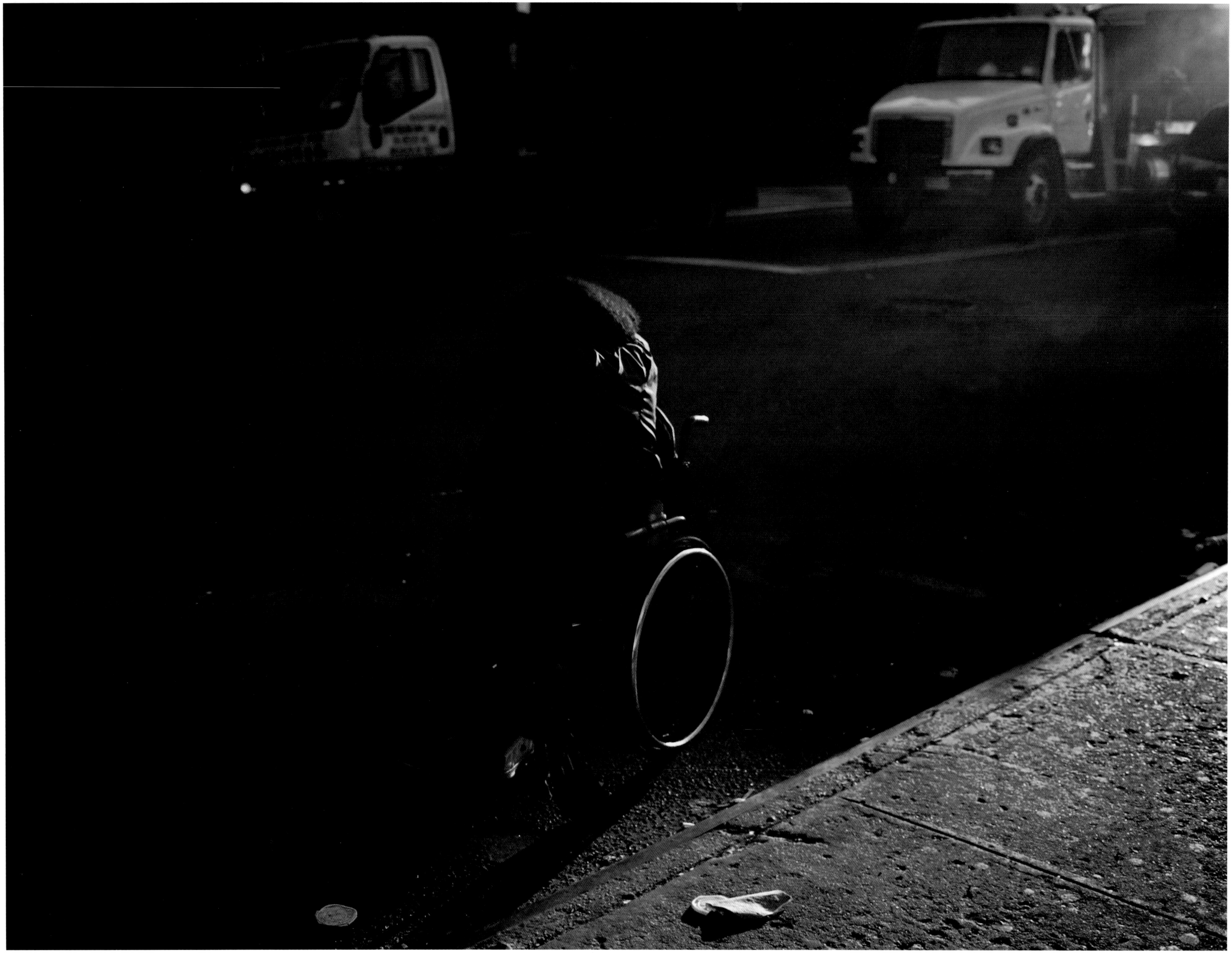

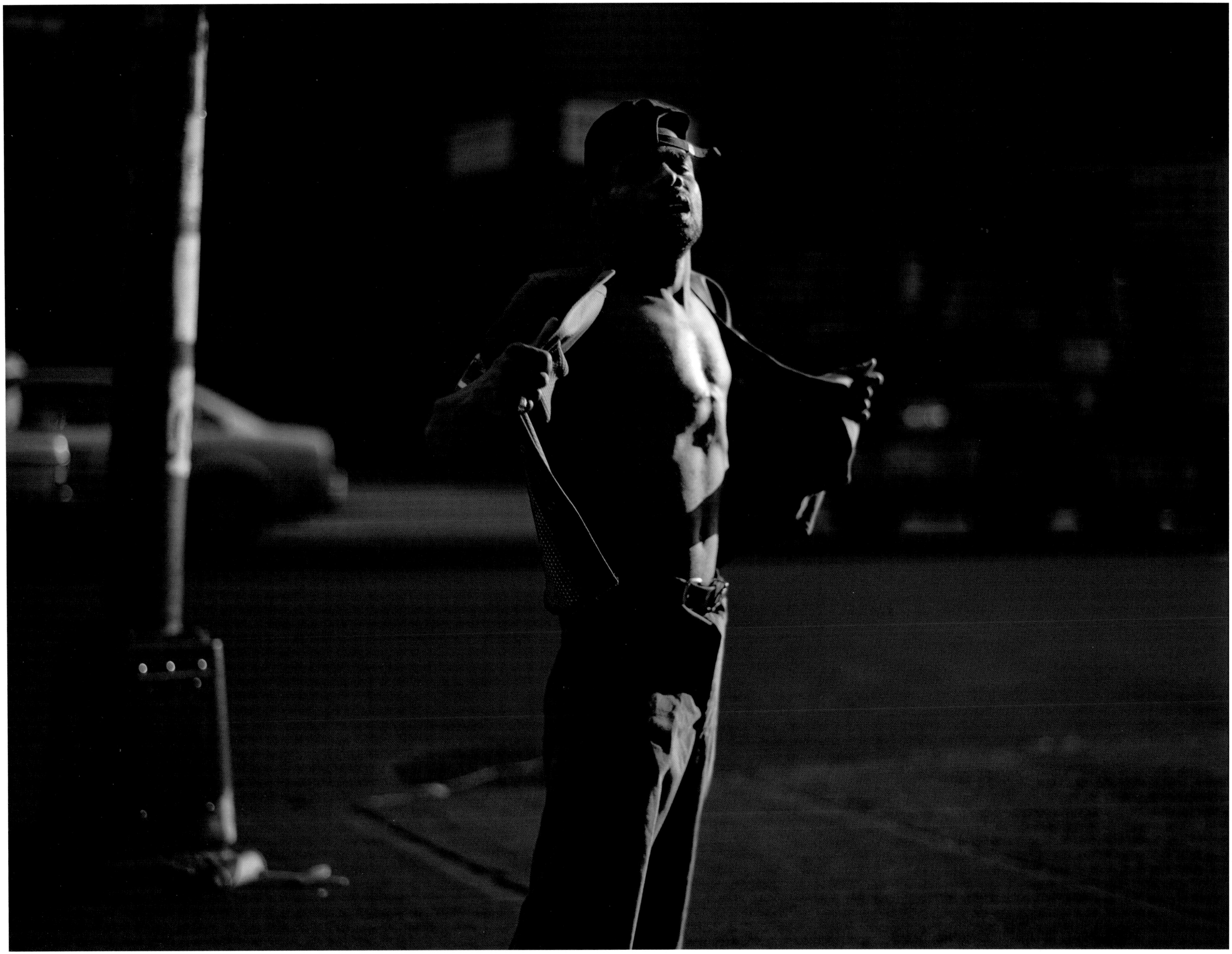

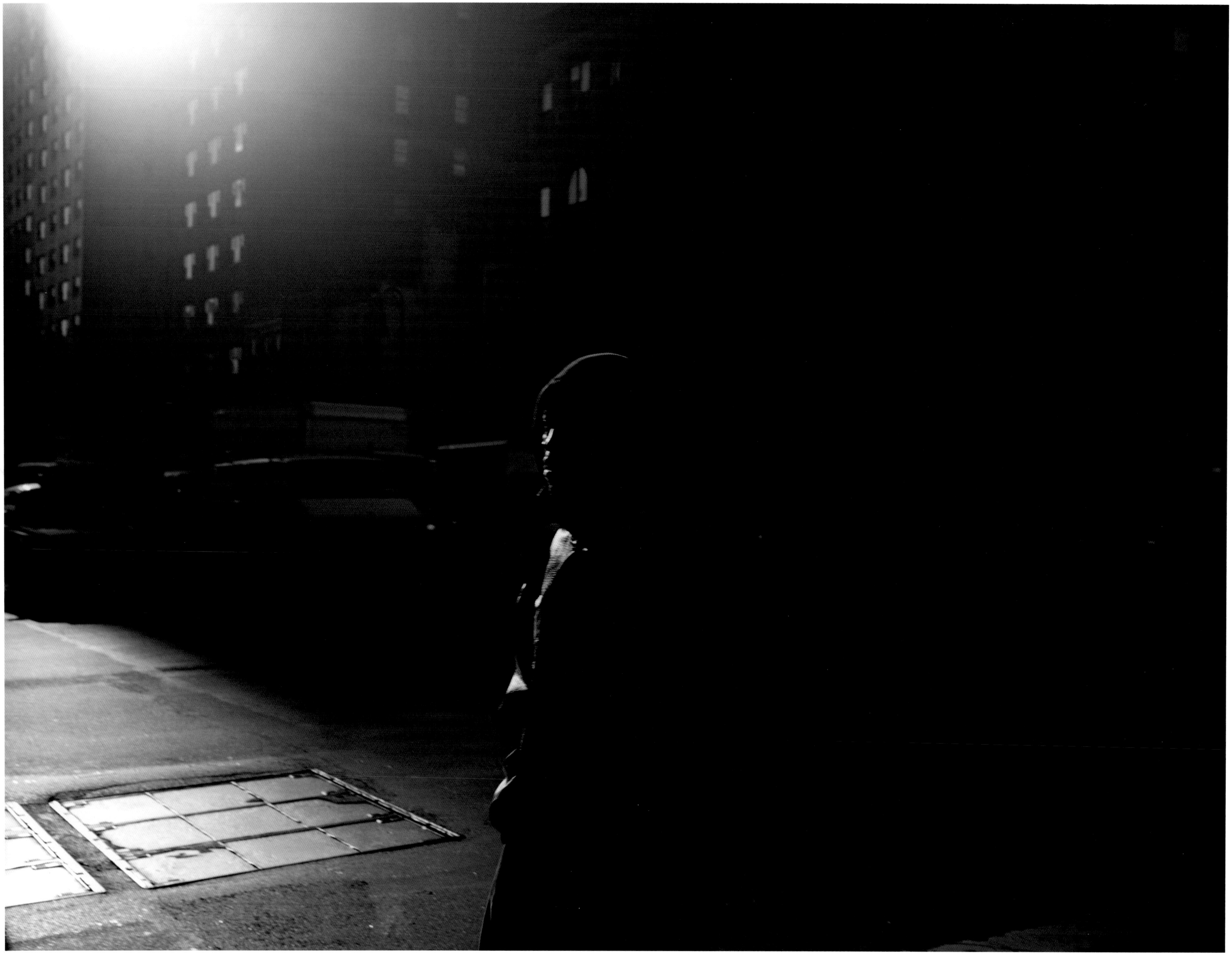

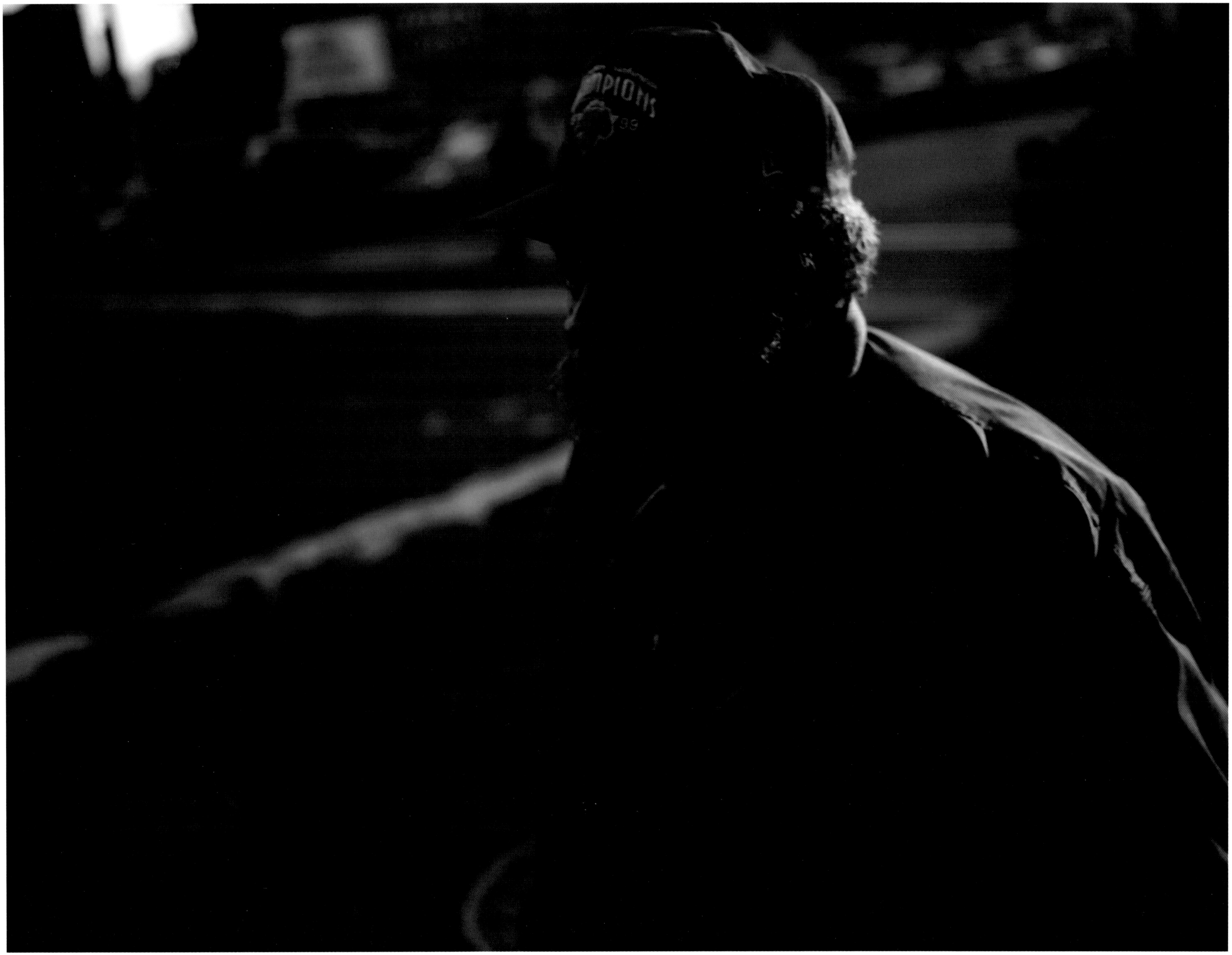

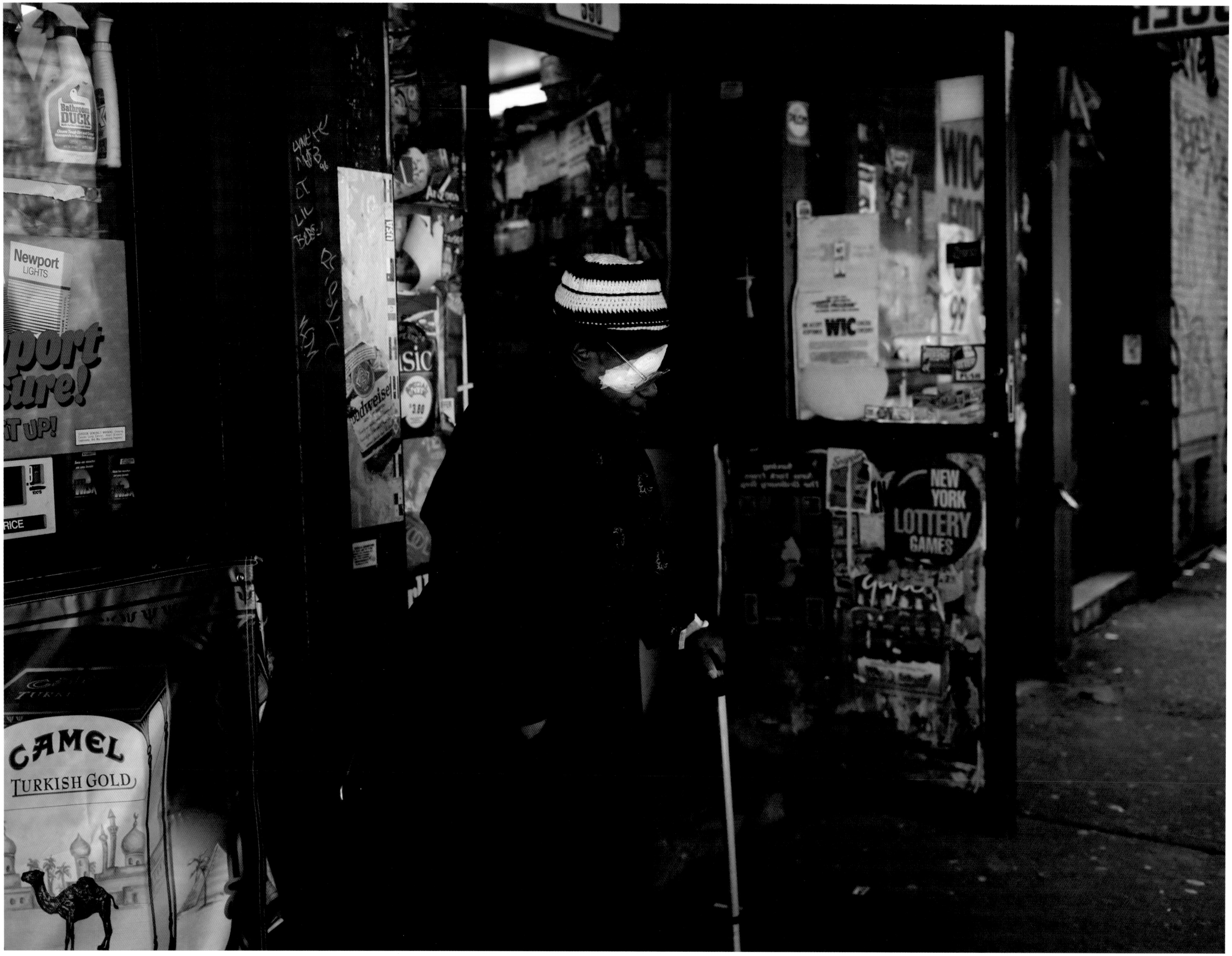
Bathroom DUCK
Newport LIGHTS
WIC
NEW YORK LOTTERY GAMES
CAMEL
TURKISH GOLD

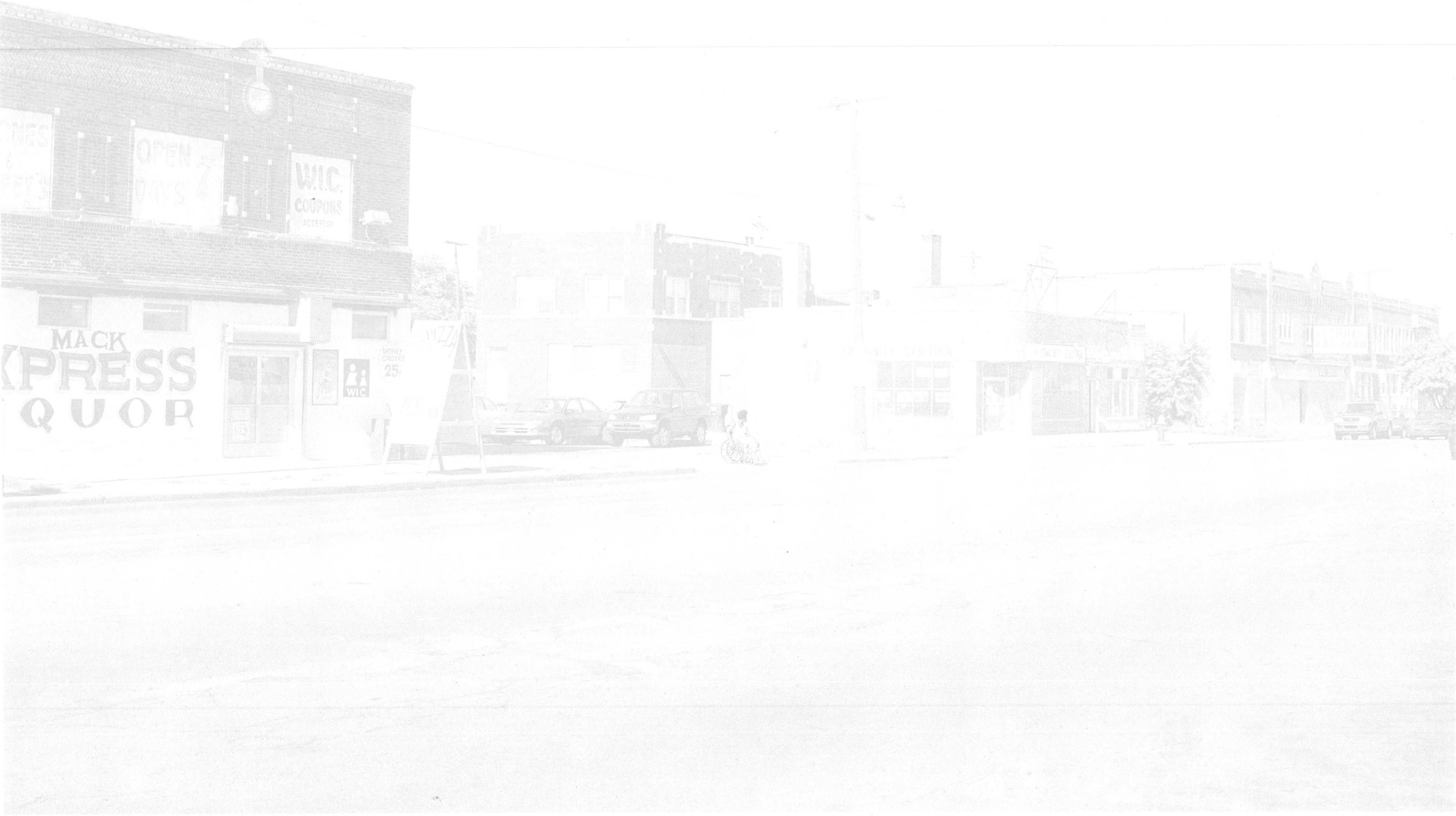

MACK
XPRESS
QUOR
OPEN
DAYS
W.I.C.
COUPONS
WIC

RAINBOW VIDEO
MOVIE RENTAL

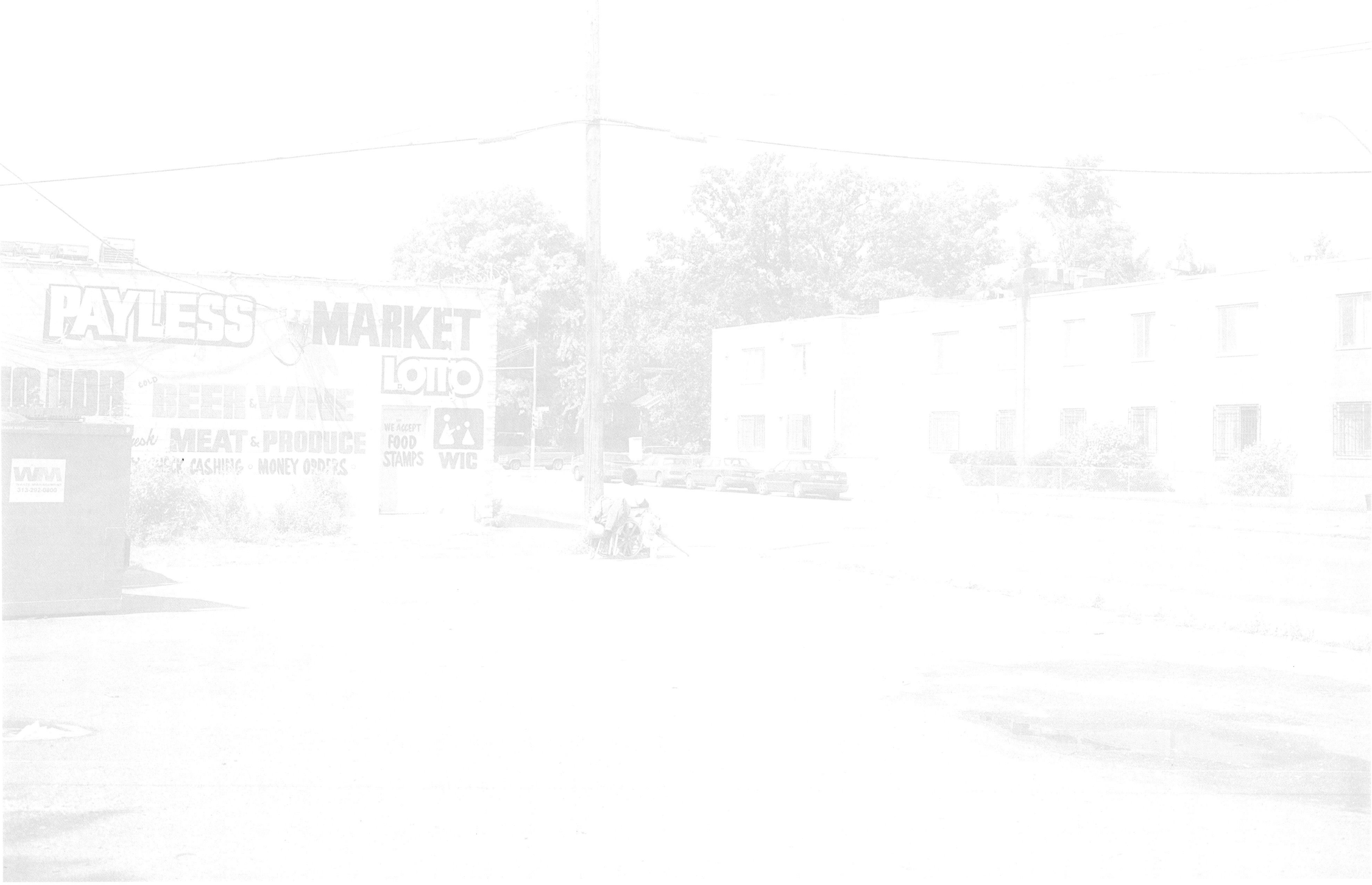
PAYLESS
MARKET
LOTTO
BEER & WINE
MEAT & PRODUCE
MONEY ORDERS
WE ACCEPT
FOOD
STAMPS
WIC

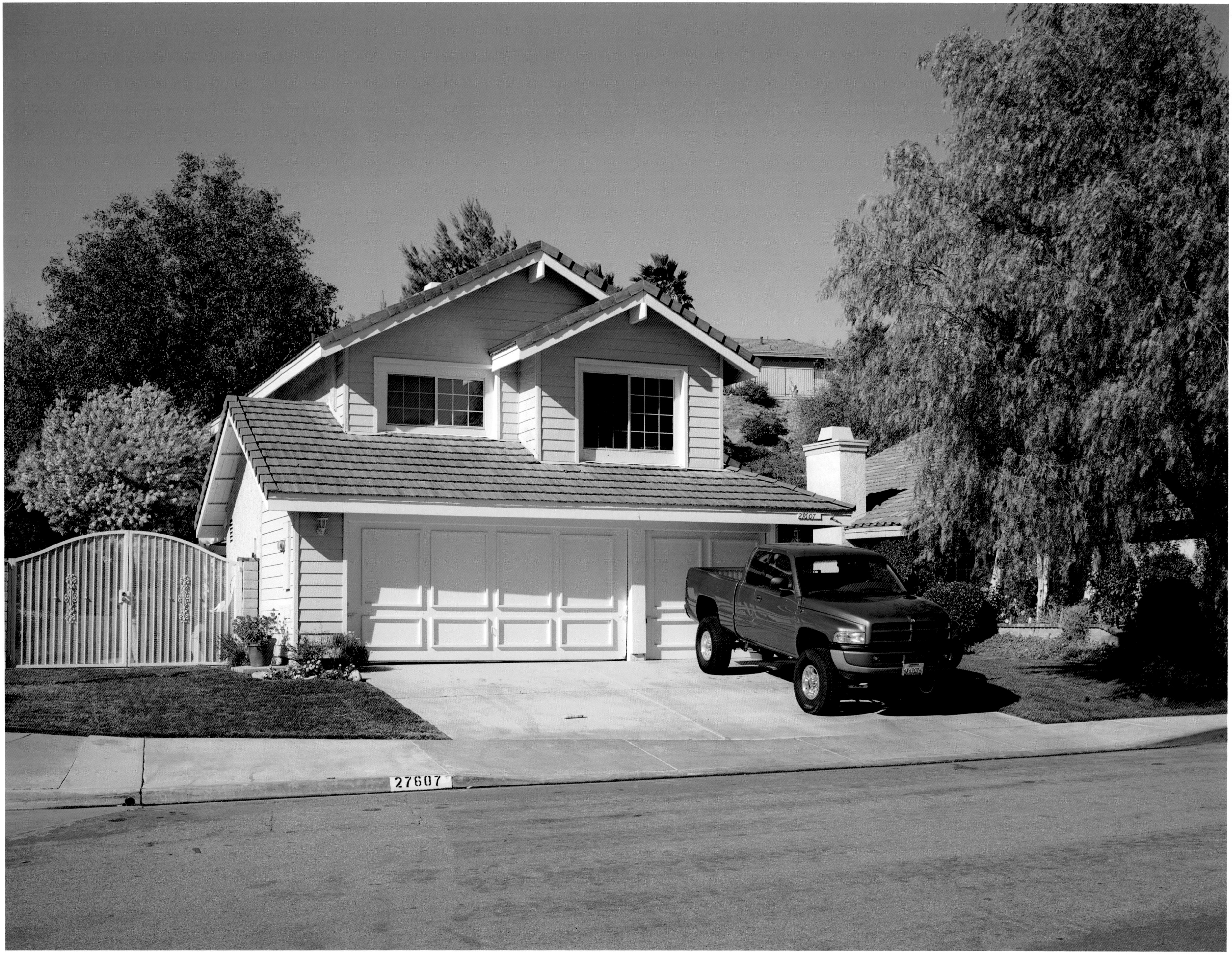
27607
27607

STOP

NO

DO NOT
ENTER
WRONG
WAY

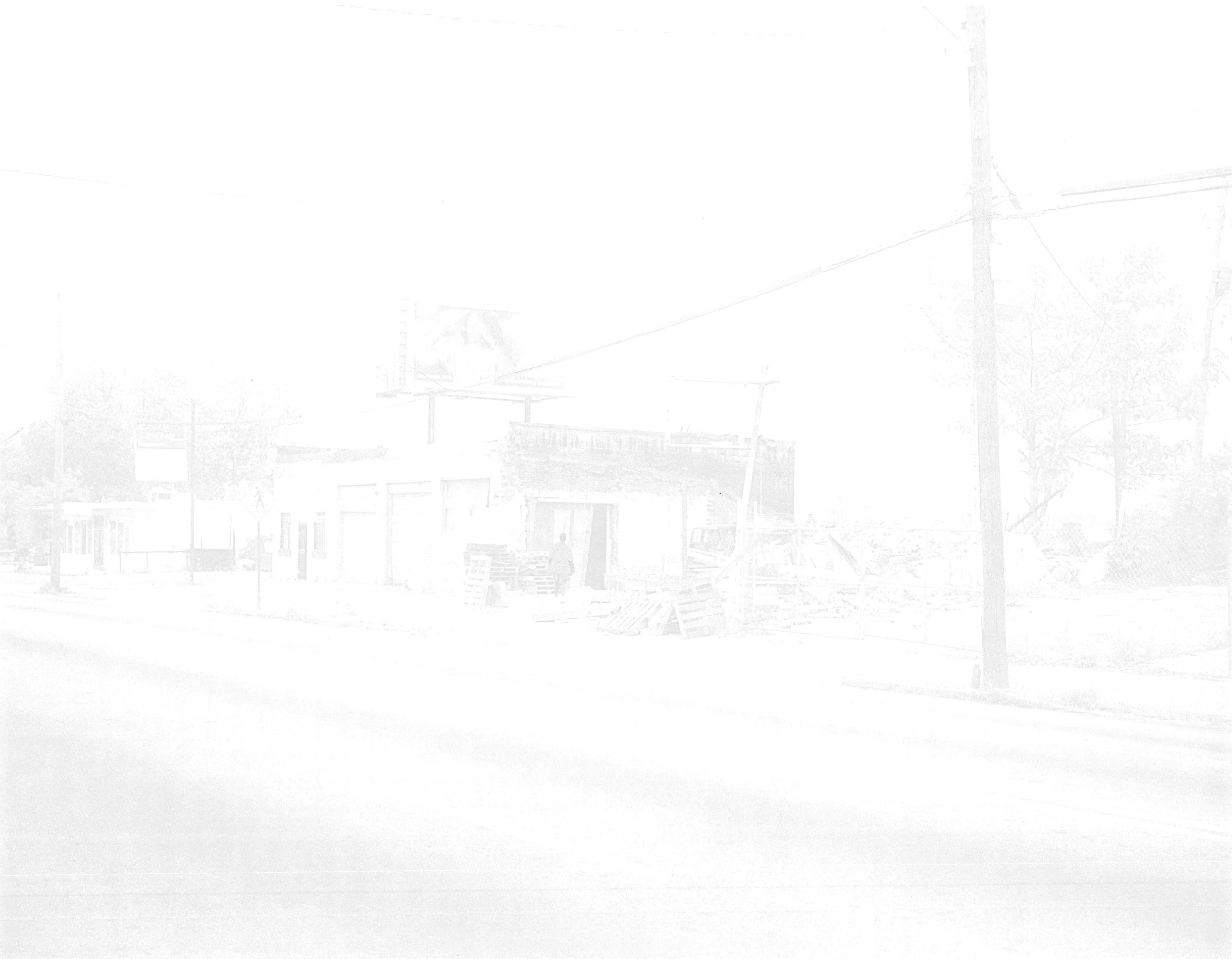

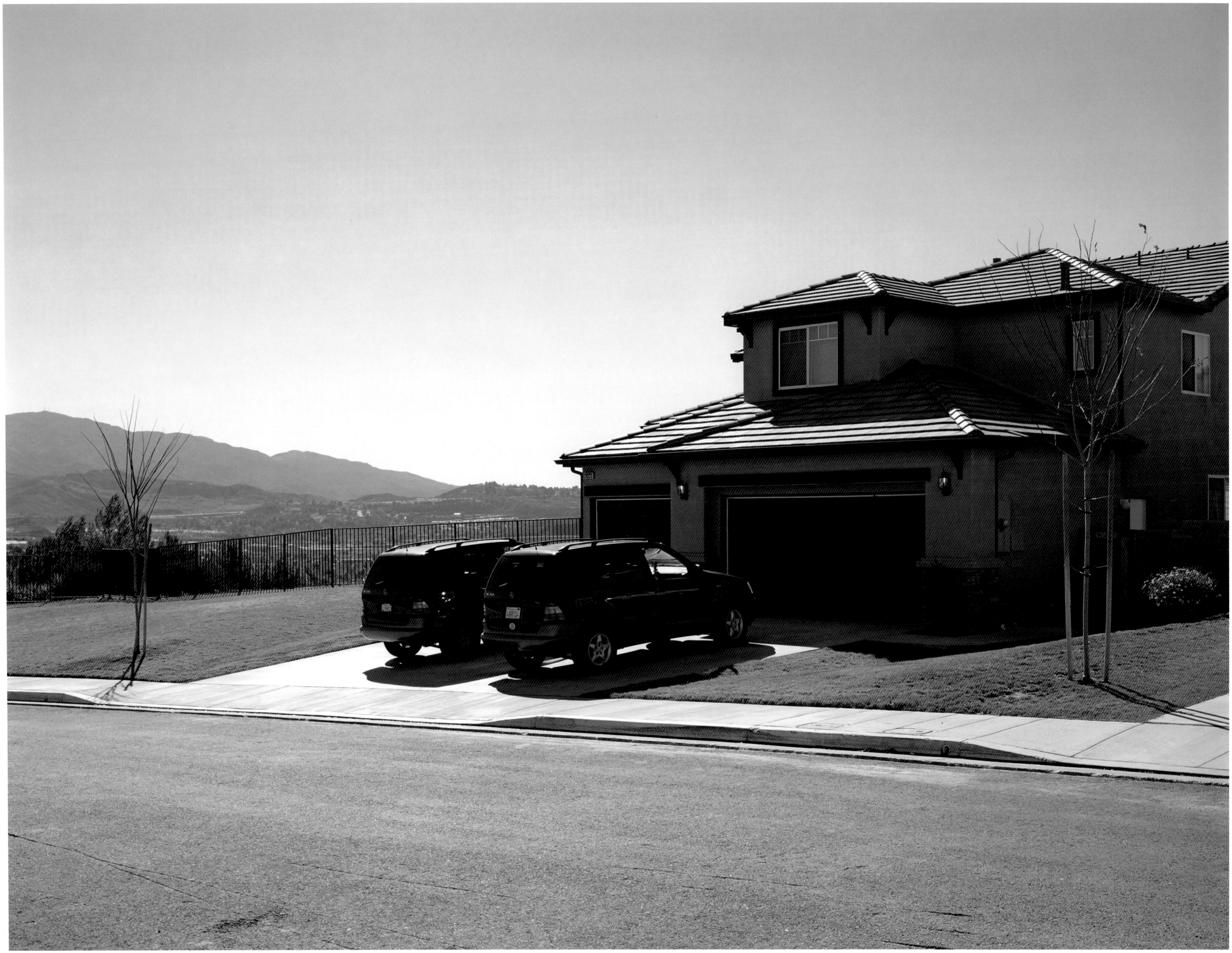

AMVETS
THRIFT
STORE
FAMILY

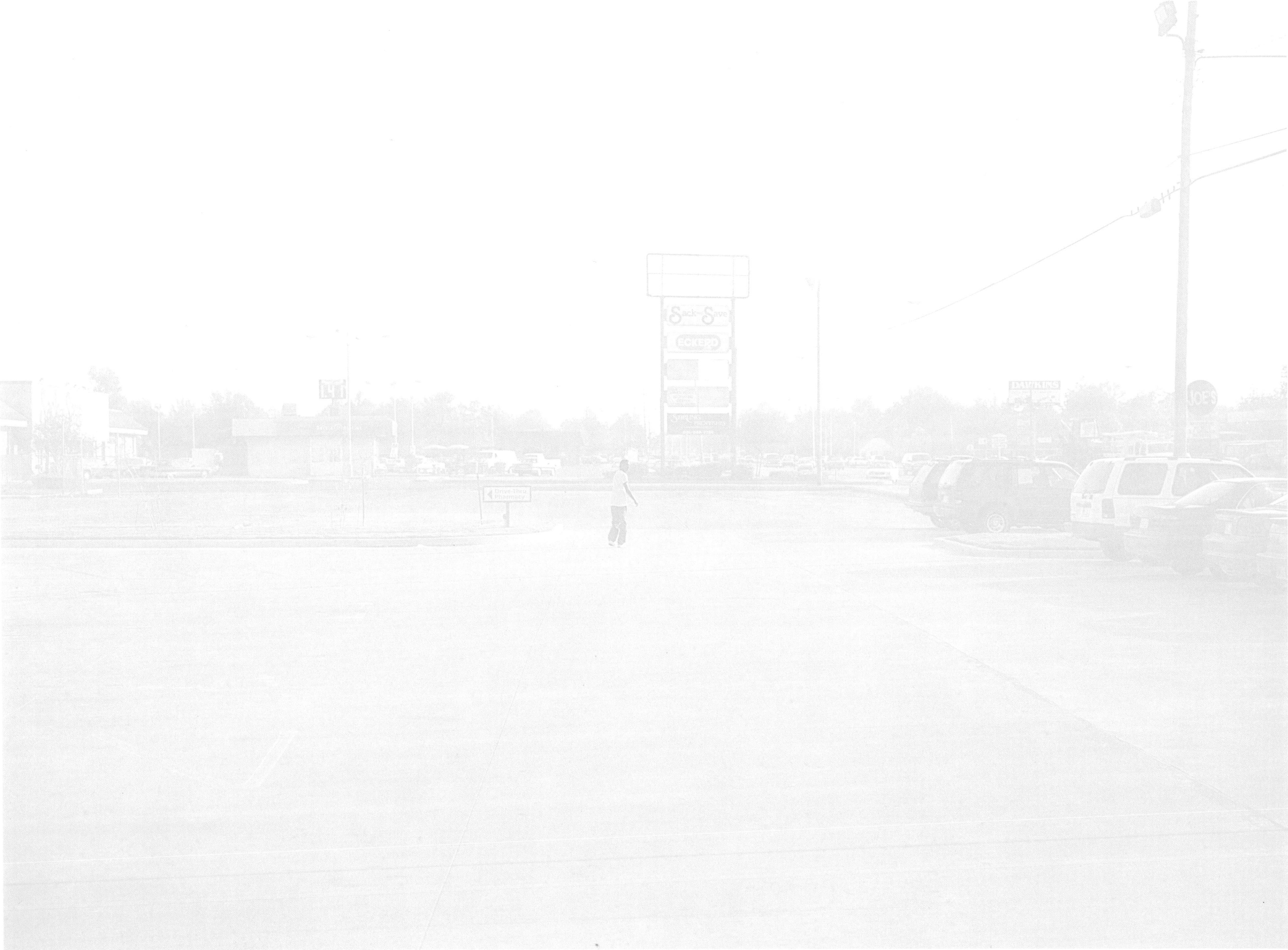
Sack-n-Save
ECKERD
Drive-Thru
Pharmacy
DAWKINS
JOE'S